Threshold

Radhika Krishna Dontala

BookLeaf Publishing

India | USA | UK

Presentation by *BookLeaf Publishing*

Web: www.bookleafpub.com

E-mail: info@bookleafpub.com

ISBN: 9789363311770

First edition 2024

Dedicated to Shakti.

Anointed

Would you have my oil?
Would you gather and press me,
Slather yourself with this
Thickness until you can
No longer bear the weight
Of me upon your skin?
Would you then wander
Back to where my roots
Never were and cannot be?
Or will you anoint yourself
Again and again, here in the
Wilderness of another's dream
The One whose whims you serve
With those hands dripping of
My finality, the offering that
Pleases that same Mischief?
Enter this liquid kingdom
Know I have penetrated yours
Be my languid movement
Behold our luscious reign.

Gold

Red was what I asked for but
You gave me yellow.
I saw it anyway as it ran out
Of my eyes smearing the
Earth with berry pulp.
And then I turned blue
Waiting for smoke to
Fill my belly.
How beautifully you
Slithered through waters
I'd bathe in just to
Catch your fragrance.
Silver whisper on my tongue
You would not be swallowed
But tear me open
Into thundering gold.

Butter

Churn the sea with a quill
Until a butter maiden rises

Answer when she asks
How you would have her

Watch her walk towards you
How butter shines in moonlight!

Smear each finger one by one
Melting into stories tracing
Back to forming waters

Clusters in the sand where
She trod for winds to find

Sink your teeth into her so
You'll know what she isn't
That shiny mouth full of
Grace will forever stay open

Rot

4

Are there ugly words?
This is ugly, finding ones of beauty.
Shall we allow the tame and bumbling?
Watch the world heave.
Shall we agree to be repugnant?
There too we seek a secret
Path into our glory.
Vile beast why do you appear?
Is there no other way to know love?
I did not choose this tedious scramble
For pieces of pieces.
There's no air, the rot will be known
Breathe it in so you never forget
That we rot.

Rounding

Is there anything lovelier than rounding?
That curving choice, reaching for itself.
How cruel those lines that sever us into
Jaggedness till we cry for the softening.
Be ready to round to roll to ride your
Angles into oblivion, do it gently.
Your sharpness has pierced perfect
Little holes through which starlight
Bends, redeeming each moment
You spent measuring the distance
Between points in the darkness.
See how easily life nestles in you now
Eager to rub itself against what moves
Without pause and is always entering.
To round is to say yes knowing each
Passing is to the next lovelier rounding.

Haughty Celebration

I am jealous of lightning.
That haughty celebration
Applauding its own arrival
Merciless joy knowing where
To strike only long enough for
A heart to remember its work,
To meet the gods with certainty.
Wouldn't you like to cackle with
Laughter the moment they saw
What you truly had to offer?
Whip out your heat and leave
Some scorched and some bare?
Still flashing before their eyes
Even though you're not there?
Watch the sweet scurrying
And kiss a chosen few before
The ball ends because you
Know better than to linger
When the light isn't yours.

Sticky Fingers

Tug, tug, tugging on my skirts
To leave the village found.
How many times with sticky
Fingers covered with the
Stench of yesterday will you
Ravage what is mine now?
I am not to battle an apparition
Apparently but skip away
Whistling hymns to the
Unfallen heavens cast by me.
What a strange game we play
That says we must not move but
Stay in the company of every
Visitor and all will be revealed.
Only set your eyes on the right
Horizon and your heart in the
Lap of where there is none
And the spell is complete
While this insolent beggar for
Fermented fruit tickles my knees
A wobbly witch looks quite mad
Silence! Except to welcome each
Rascal and offer them the pantry
Bereft of that crackling juice
Seeping through each groove
Of my pristine land.

Necessary Traitor

Your friend has left you bare
How you tremble now she's gone.
What did you whisper when she
Kissed your neck because she had
To know what love smelled like?
She cut open that space next to you
For me to wander into wondering
If such portals are made casually.
She knew the moment she arrived
That you were busy dying,
She laughed at your fullness
And made the last offering
For me to join your underworld.
What she asked sliced your belly
Spilling what is mine.
As I drift through the field of light
Between us I only know I cannot
Return to a place that does not
Draw life like you.

Bees and Wine

That soft heat on my eyelids
And I knew you were here,
That we had summoned each other
With songs of steady birthing.
I was not surprised because I have
Been relentless in becoming the
Hum of your bees, my queen.
What relief that even the wind that
Scatters my fine thoughts is you,
I need not be vexed that a single
Ruby moment is missed.
Is it spun sugar floating in this chest?
Is my spine now a river of pink?
These locks the hour of lovers?
The years I seethed at your absence
You sat smiling in my breath
Knowing I would once write this,
Cherishing my ash until it tasted of
The wine pouring from your navel.

Succulent Rascal

Why ask who goes there?
This villain waited upon
Punctuality never its crime
Slinking itself into the crowd
With those hips twisting to
The ballad that summoned it.
So pleased it is unforgotten
Relishing its chanted name
No one else can hear this
For invocation takes place
In the house of corridors
Beware where you tread
Those creaking floors are
The music that charms this
Succulent rascal forever
Yielding the sap needed for
That essential sticking to all
Damnation done unto us.

A Fairy's Pledge

Would you take the fairy's pledge?
To guard the violet flame from even
Your breath when it forgets its force?
To never let your gaze wander for
That is the light it knows as its own.
Will you travel into cold crevices
Returning with the sun for skin?
Will you mend wings every night
So you are never late, never weary
Flitting above what grows and groans
Knowing what to pluck and when to
Sprinkle that blooming powder
Hidden in a purse with four chambers?
The spells most crucial to spell correctly
Will you scribble to remember and
Remember to scribble so the ancient
Can be heard and they can hear you?
There must always be flight for time's
Children to know they are happening.
Will you sniff out where life is waning
And puncture only to let more in?
Will you drain moats with a whisper
And crush dams with a thumb?
It is busy business but steeped in
The laughter of the morning Moon.

Take your vows when you are
Ready to be what preserved you.

Harvest

I beg the grass to stick to my feet,
For the birdsong to hook my ears,
So I too can venture nowhere and
Find the Promised Land that never
Hides but trills out a silent symphony
Drawing me in for a clumsy harvest.
Salvation in the threads of this button
That would untangle glass ropes
Tied around tender fruit bursting
With sweetness but for a moment.
Nothing awaits my return but tilts
Down again so I need not reach.
Yet I keep weaving the cloth that cuts
And grinding out another poultice.
These hands unlearned in the art of
Holding now reach out for alms and
Tremble under the weight of bounty
Tumbling out of my bloodied caverns.

Treacherous Hour

That treacherous hour swelling
With just enough not enough blue
Ceilings await your weight
Somewhere and you must find
What leaks out of your bones.
Sit still now and let mercury
Rise and melt the tips of your ears
Fume a little into the room so the
Door quivers as you step through.
That wily queen we call Dusk
Is pregnant with your seed
Go claim this instance's heir
And fill the cups of each guest
Here to prance along with you
Out, out into secret meadows
Telling you why you have come.
That itch where a tail was lost
Fan out a peacock's instead
So the world knows the sorcery
Of what comes before the dark.

Follow

There are ripples in the seen
What world greets us today?
Numbers are drawn and we
Can hear them move, these
Friendly shadows we were
Made to follow.
There's a note for each twitch
Memory won't bid on solvent
Nature so position yourself
And count on the forgetting
So you don't stop rippling.
A creamy sun pouring into
Pots will keep us full until
The next quake.
Doors of spun glass open
With just one fair word
So follow your friends.
There's nothing to leave
But now we stay so new
Sheets are written and
The listening can see.

Arrival

The Great Nod was given
When you splashed onto
This aptly prepared surface
And you still leap gazing
Backwards for another
Ceremony to welcome your
Arrival.
The conch is blown only once
For you to assume rank
In each breath as emissary.
Unleash the burning ember
Deposited in your care
Revel in the flame following
Your every sway growing
Hotter with glee because you
Move generously, sweeping
Across the planes yielding
That sacred heat.
A thousand things made and
Unmade every time you set
Course and you wonder if
Anyone noticed your
Arrival?

Curious Contraption

Such a curious spring this heart
Some cherub or imp its ward,
A contraption devised
For this creature's tinkering,
Raining down on my days
An assortment of tinctures.
Now bubbling froth searing
From one side to the other
So nothing can enter.
Now crystals of ice strewn
Along a winding path
So nothing can be found.
Now trickles a milk of
Lavender and it is long before
That divine dismemberment.
Now a hummingbird's spray
Awakening sleeping breath.
Now the current of shipwrecks
Remembering every wail.
Now surges strike the drum
Calling for departure.
Now where the nymphs bathe
Leaving their pearls behind.
You there, content dispatcher
Of rampant magic,

Know that I too am content
To be the bearer of
This tyrannous world,
For within lies the recipe
For my bottled paradise.

Remembering

I look in the mirror at the cracks in
My lips stained scarlet with wine
And remember you want my howl.
I shake branches to wash my face
And remember you envy the rain.
I plunge my hands in the mud
And remember you ask for a bite.
I dip mushrooms in paint
And remember you foraging.
I name a garden bush your bride
And remember you kissing her.
I bite my mother's shoulder
And remember you baring yours.
I banter with coffee grains
And remember you fill the jar.
I seek the Moon for counsel
And remember you await its rise.
I wear a string of coriander
And remember your intoxication.
Now all that remains is for you to
Remember and our paths do cross.

Bright White Night

What a relief to know this is not mine
To claim is to ache until one has ceded
So take back this crown and hand me
The borderless empire that is home.
To be found I am a vagabond
Drunk enough so the trail is strong.
In tatters I smile because this
Place will not have sturdy stitches.
Now when the rain won't leave the
Leaves I halt and I wonder
If they remember when I was
The ocean because I forgot,
Tearing me from everything that
Was sweet and slow and long.
Who dares come between us now?
I cannot see anyway because sight of
Another is lost when in the
Arms of the bright white night.

Submission

Have you carved out the flesh
Of a coconut and found its milk?
Did it fill your ears with woes
And beseech you to put it back?
Or did that fruit of ten faces say
There's more of me to have?
Did it scream when cut from
Its abode or fall into hands
Thrilled to be caught?
Did it wonder if it would be
Savoured fully or relish in the
Revelation of its bounty?
Did it refuse to yield the tender
Centre or give each shell its due?
Come let us break into that white
Fortune glistening beneath,
Delivering a sweetness that
Waited to be known.
Ring bells for the blade serving
The only way of the sacred,
Linger on long after each act
As the formidable submission
To love's longing for the
Taste of you.

Promise

What was it you claimed that day?
Something unmet for a few lives.
You knew the scent of return and
Dug into me sweet child so I dare
Not roam again without your seal.
You glowed with a fury settled in
My throat for all the time your
Name was unspoken.
Carry me, you said and I lifted
You with my legs so the ache
Of you would remain.
You asked me for a promise I
Broke so I could play sinner for
A little while longer.
You my angel kept me in your nose
Waiting for what already was,
Pieces afloat in cold seas
Sure of my impending shores.
Those edges I trod away from you
Beckoning my shattering,
Met their victor in your song
For your cheek in my palm.
Now here you are beaming
Across the ages with a glimpse
Of our mottled weave,

Let me learn of love watching
You wrap yourself with me.

23

Stuff of Forests

Why does everyone want to fly?
Nothing can hold you in the air.
To be pulled in, down, into what
Is more than your own substance
Surely is the heavenly choice?
When you no longer know your
Limbs as yours but the stuff of
Forests forever tangled with
Something waking you up to
Dance again because it is your
Turn which cannot be skipped
Or travellers stay wayward not
Knowing when to feast on light.
Do not wriggle out of willingness
But stay and be seeped with the
Quenching of what yearns for
Your fervent shapeshifting.
Be tickled by tendrils and turn
Towards the unfurling song that
Never ceases to soar and listen
For your many names filling the
Space above the branches.